ANIMALS ON THE BRINK

Jaguars

E. Melanie Watt

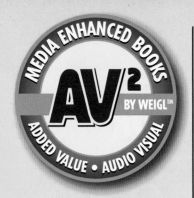

MEDIA ENHANCED BOOKS

AV²
BY WEIGL™

ADDED VALUE • AUDIO VISUAL

AV² provides enriched content that supplements and complements this book. Weigl's AV² books strive to create inspired learning and engage young minds in a total learning experience.

Your AV² Media Enhanced books come alive with...

Go to **www.av2books.com**, and enter this book's unique code.

Audio
Listen to sections of the book read aloud.

Key Words
Study vocabulary, and complete a matching word activity.

BOOK CODE

C964893

Video
Watch informative video clips.

Quizzes
Test your knowledge.

Embedded Weblinks
Gain additional information for research.

Slide Show
View images and captions, and prepare a presentation.

AV² by Weigl brings you media enhanced books that support active learning.

Try This!
Complete activities and hands-on experiments.

... and much, much more!

Published by AV² by Weigl
350 5th Avenue, 59th Floor
New York, NY 10118
Website: www.av2books.com   www.weigl.com

Library of Congress Cataloging in Publication data available upon request.
Fax 1-866-449-3445 for the attention of the Publishing Records department

ISBN 978-1-62127-222-9 (hardcover)
ISBN 978-1-62127-223-6 (softcover)

Printed in the United States of America in North Mankato, Minnesota
1 2 3 4 5 6 7 8 9 17 16 15 14 13

032013
WEP300113

Project Coordinator Aaron Carr
Design Mandy Christiansen

Every reasonable effort has been made to trace ownership and to obtain permission to reprint copyright material. The publishers would be pleased to have any errors or omissions brought to their attention so that they may be corrected in subsequent printings.

Photo Credits
Weigl acknowledges Getty Images, Alamy, and iStockphoto as photo suppliers for this title.

Contents

Take a Stand

·Debate·
Take a Stand
·Research·

The Jaguar

People sometimes think jaguars are vicious beasts that live only in the deepest, darkest jungles of South America. Jaguars are like most animals, however. They are just trying to survive in their **habitat**. Until recently, that habitat extended from North America to the southern part of South America. Jaguars often live in swampy, thick, tropical forests. This makes spotting them very difficult and studying them even more challenging. For this reason, jaguars are one of the least studied of the world's big cats. Continue reading to discover more about this fascinating animal, including how and where jaguars live, what they eat, and how their populations are at risk.

Jaguars are excellent hunters. They have sturdy bodies, sharp senses, and powerful jaws.

Unlike other big cats, jaguars spend a great deal of their time near or in water.

How to Take a Stand on an Issue

Research is important to the study of any scientific field. When scientists choose a subject to study, they must conduct research to ensure they have a thorough understanding of the topic. They ask questions about the subject and then search for answers. Sometimes, however, there is no clear answer to a question. In these cases, scientists must use the information they have to form a hypothesis, or theory. They must take a stand on one side of an issue or the other. Follow the process below for each Take a Stand section in this book to determine where you stand on these issues.

1. **What is the Issue?**
   a. Determine a research subject, and form a general question about the subject.

2. **Form a Hypothesis**
   a. Search at the library and online for sources of information on the subject.
   b. Conduct basic research on the subject to narrow down the general question.
   c. Form a hypothesis on the subject based on research to this point.
   d. Make predictions based on the hypothesis. What are the expected results?

3. **Research the Issue**
   a. Conduct extensive research using a variety of sources, including books, scientific journals, and reliable websites.
   b. Collect data on the issue and take notes on all information gathered from research.
   c. Draw conclusions based on the information collected.

4. **Conclusion**
   a. Explain the research findings.
   b. Was the hypothesis proved or disproved?

Connecting the Dots

The jaguar is the biggest cat found in North, Central, and South America.

Black jaguars have spots. The black background just makes the spots harder to see.

Features

There are many **species** of big cats. Some of them look very much alike. At first glance, the jaguar and leopard may look like the same animal. After a closer look, however, it is easy to tell one from the other. Jaguars are usually bigger than leopards. They have shorter tails and heavier bodies. Jaguars also have bigger heads, shorter legs, and larger paws compared to their bodies. These differences make jaguars look more compact and powerful but less graceful than leopards.

Another way to tell a jaguar from a leopard is by the spots on its fur. Both cats have black-outlined circles, called rosettes, on their coats. Jaguars' rosettes are usually larger. They often have one or more dots in the center. Leopards' rosettes are smaller and usually empty in the center. Jaguars and leopards are also easy to tell apart in nature because they live on different continents.

Jaguars are **mammals**. They are also the third-largest type of cat in the world. Only lions and tigers are bigger. Leopards, cougars, and cheetahs are all smaller than jaguars. The size of a particular jaguar depends on where it lives, what it eats, whether it is male or female, and how old it is. Jaguars in Central America tend to be smaller than those in Brazil. Jaguars typically stand about 27 to 29.5 inches (68 to 75 centimeters) high at the shoulders. Their tails are less than one-third of their body length. Including their tails, female jaguars are usually about 5 to 7.2 feet (1.6 to 2.2 meters) long and weigh 93 to 168 pounds (42 to 76 kilograms). This is about 11 times larger than the average **domestic** cat. Male jaguars are about 10 to 20 percent bigger than females. Males are usually 5.6 to 7.9 feet (1.7 to 2.4 m) long. They normally weigh from 126 to 220 pounds (57 to 100 kg).

Most jaguars have a golden coat that fades to white on their cheeks, throat, belly, and parts of their legs. All jaguars have rosettes as well as other spots of various sizes and shapes. The markings are larger on a jaguar's shoulders and back than on its head, neck, and legs. No two jaguars have the same pattern of spots. Not all jaguars have a golden coat. Some jaguars are **melanistic**, or black. There are also albino, or white, jaguars, but these are extremely rare.

The word *jaguar* may have come from a word in the Tupi language meaning "wild beast that overcomes its prey at a bound." The Tupi were one of the native peoples of Brazil.

Classification

Jaguars are **carnivores** and belong to the large **order** of animals called *Carnivora*. Jaguars are in the **family** of carnivores called *Felidae*, which includes all types of cats. Cats share many similarities. They have rounded heads, strong, compact bodies, whiskers, large eyes, and curved, sharp claws. All cats can hear, see, and smell very well. They also have a good sense of balance.

Jaguars are in the group, or genus, of big cats that also includes lions, tigers, and leopards. The scientific, or Latin, name for this genus is *Panthera*. All jaguars belong to the species *Panthera onca*, which includes eight different types, or subspecies. A third word follows *Panthera onca* to describe each subspecies. For example, the Peruvian jaguar is *Panthera onca peruviana*.

Extinct ancestors of the jaguar were about 20 percent bigger than jaguars today. These animals may have been bigger because they had larger animals to eat. Prehistoric remains of these extra-large jaguars have been found as far north as the U.S.-Canadian border.

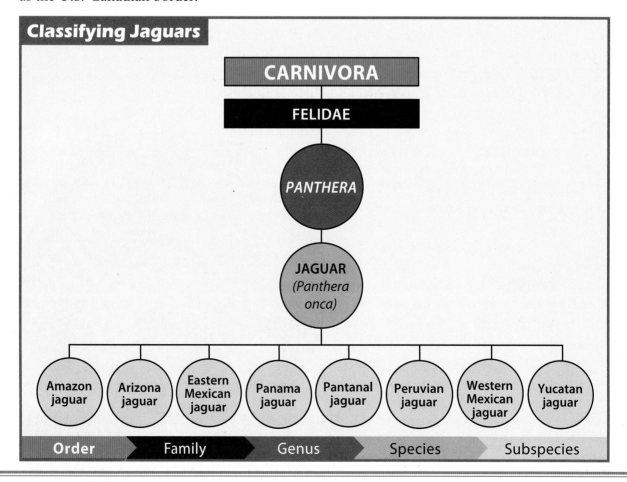

Classifying Jaguars

CARNIVORA

FELIDAE

PANTHERA

JAGUAR
(*Panthera onca*)

| Amazon jaguar | Arizona jaguar | Eastern Mexican jaguar | Panama jaguar | Pantanal jaguar | Peruvian jaguar | Western Mexican jaguar | Yucatan jaguar |

Order → Family → Genus → Species → Subspecies

Every known species and subspecies of animal has a scientific name. The scientific name for the Amazon jaguar is *Panthera onca onca*.

The Panama jaguar, which has the scientific name *Panthera onca centralis*, lives mainly in the tropical forests of Colombia.

The Pantanal jaguar is the largest of all the jaguar subspecies and can be found in Brazil.

Special Adaptations

Jaguars have many features that help them meet the challenges of their environment. A jaguar's ability to hunt and survive in its habitat depends on **adaptations** that have developed over many thousands of years.

Eyes

Jaguars, like other cats, can see in color. They use their well-developed sense of sight to help find their **prey**. They can see well both during the day and at night. Their eyes adjust very quickly to sudden darkness. This makes it easier for them to hunt when stalking through fields of tall grass, shrubs, or other plants.

Ears

Jaguars hear very well. They use their keen sense of hearing when hunting. A jaguar can find its prey by listening for the animal's movement noises. The jaguar can then creep silently toward the prey animal.

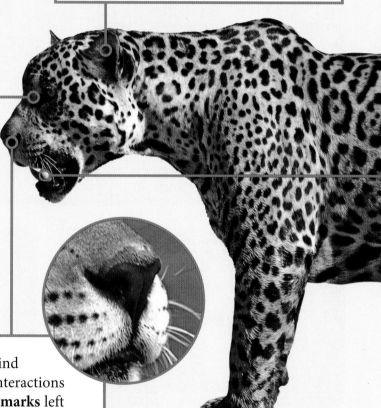

Nose

A jaguar's ability to smell can help it find prey. This sense is also important in interactions with other jaguars. Jaguars sniff **scent marks** left by other cats. These marks help a jaguar tell which other jaguars have recently been in its **home range**. From a scent mark, a jaguar can tell if another jaguar is male or female and whether it is ready to mate.

Teeth

Jaguars have 30 teeth and very powerful jaws. Compared to the size of their other teeth, their **canine** teeth are huge. These large teeth are used to successfully capture their prey. The smaller teeth are used to help chew meat.

Tail

A jaguar's tail helps keep its body balanced. This is important, especially when a jaguar walks on tree branches. The tail also helps a jaguar make quick turns while chasing prey.

Claws

Like most other cats, jaguars have **retractable claws**, which are extended only when they are being used. Jaguars use their claws to defend themselves and to hold on to their prey.

Connecting the Dots

The life span of a jaguar in nature is about 10 to 12 years. Jaguars in captivity can live for more than 20 years.

Jaguars often rest during the midday heat, though they are always on the lookout for their next meal.

Social Activities

Jaguars spend most of the time living alone. A male and female jaguar might travel together during their mating period. The pairing is only temporary, however, and they will return to their solitary lifestyle after mating.

Baby jaguars, which are called cubs, stay with their mother for up to two years. When they can take care of themselves, cubs leave to live on their own. Sometimes, cubs from the same **litter** will live together for a short time after they leave their mother.

A jaguar is active at least half of each day and uses many of its active hours to stalk prey. Jaguars are able to blend into their surroundings by either hiding under thick forest cover or resting on tree branches. They can sneak up on or lie in wait for prey and then leap to capture the animal. Jaguars prefer to use the element of surprise rather than waste energy chasing prey for long distances.

Jaguars often spend time each day grooming. They use their tongues to clean their fur. A jaguar's tongue is covered with rough bumps. This makes it a very good fur-cleaning tool. Jaguar mothers sometimes groom their cubs.

Some people who live for many years in or near jaguar home ranges never see one of these big cats. The jaguar's senses of smell, sight, and hearing are so good that it will almost always sense people and avoid contact with them before being seen. This makes tracking and studying the jaguar very difficult.

Except during mating, or in a zoo, it is very rare for adult jaguars to spend time together.

Communication

Jaguars have many ways of communicating with one another. This communication is usually not face-to-face. Jaguars most often send and receive information from a distance.

Some people describe jaguar **vocalizations** as sounding like snoring noises or coughs. A jaguar usually makes three or more short, hoarse coughs in a row. Since the sounds travel a long way, jaguars tend to seem closer than they really are when they make these calls. Calls can be a way of communicating whether a jaguar is male or female or finding out if there are any other jaguars nearby. A female often calls when she is searching for a mate. A male answers back until they find each other.

Some jaguars flatten grass and other vegetation to make bedding sites. They may mark these areas by urinating to leave scent marks. Jaguars also make **scrapes**. These are places where they scrape up a patch of earth with their paws. Jaguars sometimes rake, or scratch, tree trunks. Scrapes and scratches on trees are thought to be other ways that a jaguar communicates with other cats. These signs tell other jaguars that the location has already been claimed. Jaguars are not the only big cats to scratch tree trunks. Cougars, tigers, and leopards also rake tree trunks with their claws.

The jaguar's whiskers also help it gather information. The whiskers have sensitive nerve endings. They "feel" objects on either side of them while the animal is moving through thick brush at night.

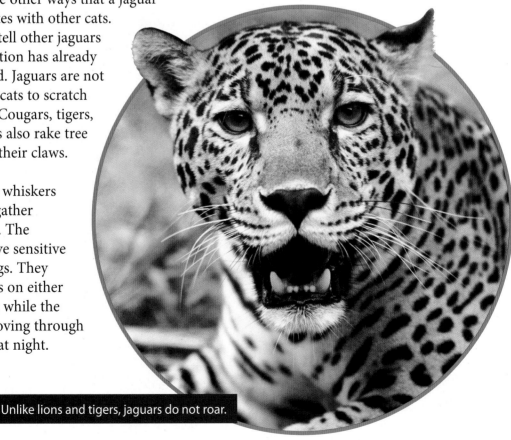

Unlike lions and tigers, jaguars do not roar.

Very small scrapes are sometimes found beside larger ones. This suggests that scraping is one of the skills a mother teaches her cubs.

A jaguar's claws stay sharp partly because it keeps them retracted until they are needed. This helps jaguars to use their claws to mark trees in their territories.

Body Language

In addition to using sounds, scrapes, and scratches on trees to communicate, jaguars also use body language. Jaguars behave in much the same way as other big cats when they are aggressive or defensive. They may use their body posture or facial expressions to display how they are feeling. Watching a jaguar's tail is also a good way of telling the animal's mood. A motionless tail tends to indicate that the cat is relaxed. When a jaguar swishes its tail rapidly, this is a sign that the animal is feeling anxious.

Submission

Jaguars that are defensive, or submissive, flatten their ears back tightly against their heads. Their pupils enlarge, and they often flatten themselves against the ground or back away low to the ground. Submissive jaguars may even roll over on their backs.

Friendly

When adult male and female jaguars are being friendly they sometimes rub their necks together or lie close to each other. This usually happens only when the jaguars are mating.

Aggression

Jaguars on the offensive hold their ears forward and stand up with their weight mostly on their front legs. They may also display their teeth and vocalize in an attempt to scare other jaguars.

Closeness

Jaguars, like all other cats, use their tongues to clean their fur. Mother jaguars will use their tongues to clean their infants. This also helps to develop a sense of closeness.

Is it right to keep jaguars in zoos?

Zoos around the world house thousands of different animals, allowing people to view them in a safe and secure setting. Visitors to zoos hope to catch a glimpse of animals that they may never get the opportunity to see in nature. Many of these zoos work hard to help save **threatened** and **endangered** species. However, some people argue that it is cruel to keep animals such as jaguars away from their natural habitat and confined to a small area.

FOR

1. Many zoos help care for injured wildlife. They also participate in breeding programs to help ensure the survival of a species.
2. Zoos are ideal places to study animals. They provide scientists with a safe environment to conduct their research.

AGAINST

1. Jaguars are used to roaming large areas and should not be kept in a small, enclosed environment.
2. Jaguars, like other animals found in zoos, may lose their abilities to survive in nature once they grow accustomed to being taken care of by humans.

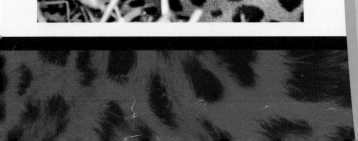

Connecting the Dots

A mother will not let other jaguars near her cubs, not even the cubs' father.

Finding a mate is not an easy matter. Sometimes, jaguars must travel great distances before they come across a suitable partner.

Mating and Birth

The only time that jaguars meet with other adult jaguars is during mating. Jaguars mate in nature throughout the year. During periods of mating, a male jaguar may travel beyond its home range in order to increase the likelihood of finding a female. Males competing for the attention of a female may be aggressive toward each other in a display of dominance.

The male and female jaguar are together only briefly during mating. The **gestation period** for jaguars is about 13 weeks long. Male jaguars do not help protect the pregnant female or assist in raising the young. In fact, a father jaguar has no contact with the young cubs. The mother jaguar gives birth to the cubs alone and raises them all by herself. There are usually two to three cubs in a litter.

Female jaguars are very protective of their young. They will defend their cubs against anything that might try to harm them. There are many animals, such as large snakes and caimans, that are capable of eating the newborn cubs.

If not out hunting for food for her young family, a mother jaguar will spend most of the day near her cubs.

Cubs

Jaguar cubs are small and fragile when they are born, but they soon become playful and curious about their world. For up to two years, their mother will protect the cubs and feed them. She will also teach them the skills they will need to survive, such as how to hunt.

When the young are old enough, they leave their mother and find their own territories. Only then does the mother mate again and raise new cubs. The cubs will not produce young of their own until they are about 3 years old.

When very young, jaguar cubs have long, bushy, spotted coats. As the cubs get older, their small spots grow larger, and some spots develop into rosettes. Cubs that are born with a light golden coat darken slightly in color as they age. Golden and black jaguars were once thought to be different subspecies. Now, scientists know that they are not, since they can both be found in the same litter.

The mother often hides her cubs in a den until they are about 2 months old. The den may be in bushes or other vegetation, in a cave, between rocks, under a fallen log, beneath burrowed out tree roots, or under a riverbank. She hunts near the den until the cubs are old enough to travel. Mothers **nurse** their young and provide them with food from the hunt.

Like other mammals, jaguar mothers nurse their young with milk produced from their bodies.

On average, a female jaguar will have about eight or nine cubs during her lifetime.

Connecting the Dots

For cubs, playing is a way to learn hunting and survival skills. Cubs often play with their teeth showing and their claws extended.

Although jaguar cubs have sharp teeth and claws, they are careful not to cause any harm during playtime.

Development

Small and helpless at birth, jaguar cubs are about 16 inches (40 cm) long and weigh about 28 ounces (800 grams). For the first few days after the cubs are born, the mother rarely leaves the den. The cubs at this age cannot even make the meow sound that is common in older cats. Instead they make bleating noises, similar to the sounds a sheep might make. The cubs grow quickly, gaining about 1.7 ounces (48 g) per day for the first 50 days. Cubs are usually born with their eyes closed. After about a week, they open their eyes. The cubs first walk at about 18 days of age.

Jaguar cubs are able to follow their mother when they are between 6 and 8 weeks old. They remain in the den for about 8 weeks. By this time, the cubs have developed good climbing skills. When the cubs are about 10 weeks old, they begin to eat meat, but they will continue to drink their mother's milk for several more months.

The cubs continue to play and explore. This helps to improve the coordination and other skills that they will later need to hunt successfully. At about 15 weeks, the cubs' bleating cries turn into meowing sounds. Their calls get deeper with age until the animals are about 1 year old, when they begin to sound like adults.

By the fourth or fifth month, the cubs drink much less of their mother's milk. They eat mostly meat. By the cubs' seventh month, the spots and colors of their coats lose their cublike look and become their permanent adult markings. Once they are old enough to live in their own territories, jaguars often settle far away from where they were born.

Jaguar cubs tend to be curious animals and will spend most of their day playing and exploring the world around them.

Habitat

Jaguars can live in many different types of habitats, including rainforests, marshlands, and grasslands. They are usually found in places that have plant cover, water, and many other animals for them to eat. Jaguars found in nature today are mostly located in and around the Amazon River basin. This vast region includes parts of many South American countries, including Bolivia, Brazil, Colombia, Ecuador, Guyana, Peru, and Venezuela. Smaller populations of jaguars are also found in other South American countries, as well as in parts of Central America and Mexico. Although jaguars spend much of their time near rivers, swamps, or other good sources of water, they are quite adaptable. Jaguars have been seen in deserts and on mountains at an altitude higher than 8,800 feet (2,700 m) above sea level.

Organizing the Tropical Forest

Earth is home to millions of different **organisms**, all of which have specific survival needs. These organisms rely on their environment, or the place where they live, for their survival. All plants and animals have relationships with their environment. They interact with the environment itself, as well as the other plants and animals within the environment. These interactions create **ecosystems**.

Ecosystems can be broken down into levels of organization. These levels range from a single plant or animal to many species of plants and animals living together in an area.

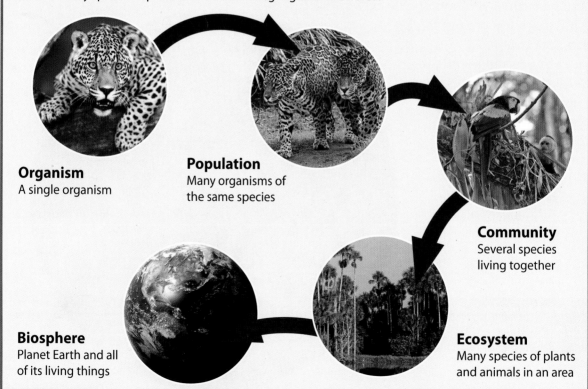

Organism
A single organism

Population
Many organisms of
the same species

Community
Several species
living together

Ecosystem
Many species of plants
and animals in an area

Biosphere
Planet Earth and all
of its living things

Connecting the Dots

Today, jaguars are almost never seen in the United States, but scientists found one in Arizona in 2009.

Jaguars tend to do best in places where there are few or no humans. Some people are afraid of jaguars and will try to harm any jaguar they see.

Connecting the Dots

A male jaguar will not usually allow another male inside its home range.

Jaguars are very good climbers. Their sharp claws help them grip and hold on to the rough bark on trees.

Range

Within its home range, a jaguar eats, finds mates, and interacts with other jaguars. The size of the home range depends on the habitat. Some parts of a larger home range might not be used much, such as a lake, where jaguars would mainly use the banks and the shallow waters. The size of the home range also depends on how many and what types of prey animals are available. Larger home ranges are found in areas where prey is less common. In these cases, the jaguar needs a larger area in which to search for food.

The size of a home range also depends on whether the jaguar is male or female. Female jaguars raise their young within a home range that is usually about 10 to 15 square miles (25 to 40 square kilometers). The home ranges of male jaguars are twice this size. A male jaguar's territory often overlaps the home ranges of one or more females. Except during mating, jaguars are able to avoid one another by long-distance communication. In this way, they can use the same areas but at different times.

Jaguars spend part of the day resting. This is usually done under the cover of trees or large-leaf plants. The rest of the day is spent hunting and patrolling their territory.

Young jaguars must keep moving through other jaguar territories until they find a home of their own.

Jaguars can swim across rivers as wide as 330 feet (100 m). They have even been seen hauling heavy prey out of deep waters.

Seasonal Activities

There are usually two main seasons in jaguar habitats. They are the rainy season and the dry season. In the rainy season, areas of a jaguar's territory may not be usable because of flooding. This means that many jaguars have much smaller territories during the rainy season. The jaguar's prey are also often crowded into these smaller areas at this time of year. This makes them easier to find.

Jaguar eating habits change throughout the year. Some foods, such as turtle or iguana eggs, are available only part of the time. Some of the jaguar's prey may be easier to catch at a particular time of year. For example, during nesting season, the turtles are easy to catch when they climb out of the water to lay their eggs on the beach. Many prey species tend to have young in one season and not in the other. Some jaguar prey may also be easier to catch when they are protecting their young. In the case of larger prey animals, jaguars may prefer hunting the young, rather than trying to take an adult animal.

As the largest predator, the jaguar plays an important role in maintaining the balance of its ecosystem. By controlling the population of prey animals, jaguars keep their habitats healthy. They keep prey from eating too much of an area's plants and small animals.

From an Expert

"With each passing year, the forests that shelter and protect these magnificent beasts shrink further and further before man's relentless encroachment."
- Peter G. Crawshaw, Jr.

Peter G. Crawshaw, Jr., is a biologist who has spent years studying jaguars and other wildlife in the Pantanal, a wetlands area in southwestern Brazil.

Diet

Jaguars hunt and eat other animals as their main source of food. They also eat a small amount of vegetation, including grass, to help them digest food. Though jaguars are large, many of the animals they prey upon are relatively small. Prey animals can include lizards and small mammals such as mice. Jaguars' diets vary depending on what types of prey are available in the areas where they live.

Jaguars are opportunistic feeders. This means they eat almost any reasonably sized animal they come across. One of the jaguar's favorite foods in South America is an animal called the capybara. Capybaras are the

Capybaras can weigh up to 175 pounds (80 kg).

world's largest rodents. In some parts of South America, capybaras can make up a large part of a jaguar's diet. However, capybaras are not found in all parts of the jaguar's range. Jaguars in other areas must eat more of other types of animals. Jaguars eat many species of reptiles. Their favorite reptile prey include caimans, turtles, and iguanas.

Although jaguars usually hunt live prey, they will also eat carrion, or dead animals. What an individual jaguar eats depends on what it finds while hunting. It may also depend on what the jaguar has become accustomed to eating or is good at catching. A jaguar's diet is likely to change with the animal's age. Young jaguars might not be as skilled at catching larger or more difficult prey.

Jaguars often scoop fish out of the water with their paws. To catch turtles, jaguars sometimes turn them over on their backs. This gives a jaguar easy access to the animal's soft flesh, avoiding the hard turtle shell. Jaguars may pounce on large prey, such as the capybara, and use its powerful jaws to take the animal. A jaguar may also stun its prey by simply hitting it on the head with a front paw.

Once it has taken its prey, a jaguar will often drag the body a long way to a protected area to eat. People have observed jaguars dragging full-grown horses and cows more than 650 yards (600 m). Though this practice is not nearly as common, jaguars will sometimes carry large animals up into trees to eat them.

Connecting the Dots

Most people think that jaguars are active only at night. Research now shows that jaguars are often quite active during daylight hours as well. They even hunt during the day, though most jaguars seem to be most active at dusk.

Jaguars are known to sneak up on their prey quietly.

The Food Cycle

A food cycle shows how energy in the form of food is passed from one living thing to another. Jaguars have been reported to eat more than 85 different prey species, including mammals, reptiles, birds, and fish. As they feed, jaguars affect the lives of other living things and the environment that they live in. The diagram below displays the flow of energy from one living thing to the next through a **food web**.

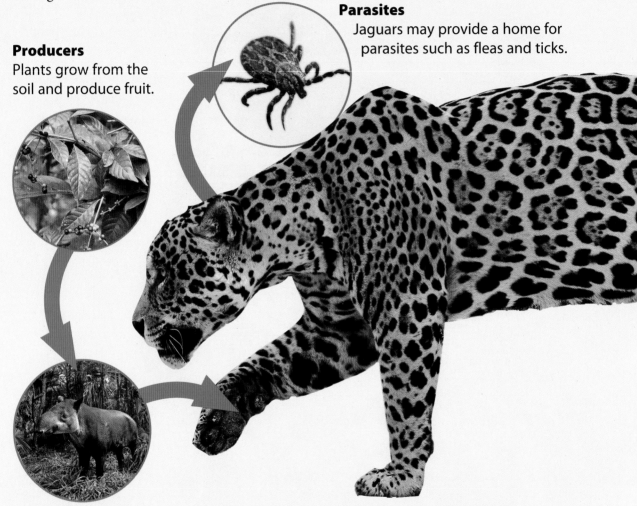

Parasites
Jaguars may provide a home for parasites such as fleas and ticks.

Producers
Plants grow from the soil and produce fruit.

Primary Consumers
Animals such as the tapir and capybara will eat the plants and fruit.

Secondary Consumers
Jaguars eat many types of animals and provide food for other living things.

Tertiary Consumers

Animals such as vultures will feed on the body of a dead jaguar.

Decomposers

When a jaguar dies, decomposers in the soil will break down the body, adding nutrients to the soil.

Debate · Take a Stand · Research

Is it a good idea to reintroduce jaguars into former habitats?

Not long ago, the jaguar made its home in the southwestern United States. Jaguars were spotted in Texas until the middle of the 20th century. Should scientists reintroduce jaguars into one or more of their historic habitats?

FOR

1. Reintroducing jaguars into regions that were once part of their natural habitat may help improve their chances for survival as a species.
2. Scientists will be able to gain a better understanding of jaguars by studying them in all of their natural habitats.

AGAINST

1. Jaguars can pose a threat to humans and domestic animals living in what was once their historic habitat.
2. Reintroducing a jaguar population to a certain area may negatively affect the current balance of the local ecosystem.

Connecting the Dots

In every country where jaguars live, cougars can also be found. Even though cougars are likely to compete for some of the same prey as jaguars, the two species seem to avoid one another.

Jaguars use their strong sense of smell to keep out of areas occupied by other jaguars. This helps them avoid direct confrontations.

Competition

Even though jaguars are big, powerful predators, they do not always win their competitions with prey. Jaguars may be hurt when they are stabbed, scratched, or bitten by an animal they are hunting, or when they are trampled by larger prey. Jaguars that hunt poisonous snakes or porcupines can be injured by these prey animals as well.

Jaguars rarely fight with other jaguars. They usually avoid one another as much as possible. In very rare cases, however, jaguars have eaten other jaguars. Why or when they might do this is unknown. Scientists know it has happened because a few males that have been studied were found to have other jaguars' remains in their stomachs.

With its strong teeth and powerful jaws, a jaguar can easily chew through the tough skin of a caiman.

From an Expert

"The jaguar...is now threatened not only by skin hunters and habitat destruction, but also by the extinction of many of its prey, every species of which is intensively hunted by humans."
- Louise Emmons

Louise Emmons is a biologist who has spent years studying jaguars, cougars, and ocelots in the rainforests of Peru.

Jaguars and Humans

Humans are by far the biggest threat to jaguars. In some countries, jaguars are not protected by law. This often means that jaguars are shot on sight. People sometimes shoot jaguars because they are afraid of these big cats. However, jaguars are the only big cats that never develop the habit of attacking people, so they are not a real threat.

During the peak fur-trading years in the 1960s, thousands of jaguars were taken so that their skins could be used to make coats.

Other people shoot jaguars because they want their skins. In most areas, jaguar skins can no longer be legally traded because jaguars are protected by laws. Some people hunt jaguars because they are trying to protect their domestic animals. Although jaguars sometimes take domesticated animals, such as cattle, they are responsible for only a very small percentage of all deaths of such animals. Humans may even cause jaguars to hunt domestic animals by overhunting many of the prey species that jaguars prefer. When this happens, jaguars must switch to other prey, which may include cattle or other livestock.

As long as humans continue to view jaguars as a threat, the future of these animals remains uncertain.

Take a Stand

Debate · *Research*

Should jaguars be destroyed if they are thought to take livestock?

In many countries, ranchers are legally allowed to hunt a jaguar if they think the jaguar has taken their livestock. Some people argue that ranchers have a right to protect the animals in their care. Other people think saving a vanishing species is more important than protecting the small number of domestic animals put at risk by jaguars.

FOR

1. Jaguars that begin taking cattle may switch completely from preying on wildlife to preying only on cattle. One jaguar was thought to have preyed on cattle one hundred times in two years.
2. Cattle should be the priority, especially in developing countries, where people urgently need the food and money that their herds produce.

AGAINST

1. Some jaguars do prey on cattle, but many are blamed for taking cattle that they did not harm. This may happen when cattle die from other causes, such as broken legs or disease, and then a jaguar feeds on the carcass.
2. Jaguars should be the priority because they are decreasing in numbers throughout their range. A solution could be to pay ranchers for any cattle lost to a jaguar.

Folklore

Jaguars were common in the folklore and religions of Central and South American native cultures. Jaguars were worshiped by cultures that include the Aztec, Maya, Olmec, and Zapotec. For many of these peoples, jaguars meant terror and mystery, but also strength, nobility, and bravery. Jaguars were also thought to have magical and healing powers.

In the Mayan religion, the god who rules the world is a jaguar. The Mayan word for "jaguar," *balam*, can also mean "priest." The Temple of the Giant Jaguar in Guatemala was built by the Maya about 1,300 years ago. The Maya believed that solar eclipses were caused by the jaguar eating the Sun.

In the Aztec religion, several gods, including the god of the night sky and the rain god, were represented as jaguars. The best Aztec warriors belonged to either the order of the eagle or the order of the jaguar. Jaguars played an even more important role in the Olmec culture. The Olmec formed a jaguar cult. Their art often showed "were-jaguars," creatures that were half-human and half-jaguar.

In South American folktales, jaguars are sometimes described as helpful, dangerous, or even misunderstood. They are often said to be great hunters. In many tales, the jaguar is seen as a magical part of the jungle.

The Temple of the Giant Jaguar, located in Tikal, Guatemala, was built as a tomb for a Mayan ruler.

Myth	**VS**	Fact

Jaguars often stalk humans, intending to attack them.

Jaguars follow humans and other animals that travel through their territories. This habit led to the belief that jaguars are a danger to humans. The animals' tendency to follow most likely means that jaguars are curious about anything new in their territories. Jaguars never develop the habit of regularly attacking humans.

Jaguars use their tails to catch fish.

This is not really true but may not be completely false. Some people have seen jaguars sitting over the edge of the water scooping fish out with their paws. They noticed that the jaguar's tail would sometimes flick around on the surface of the water while the jaguar looked for fish. This movement on the surface of the water might help attract fish.

Jaguars do not like to get wet.

Domestic cats have a reputation for avoiding water, but jaguars enjoy the water. They often cool off by standing or lying down in rivers or other bodies of water during the heat of the day. Jaguars swim very well. They always keep at least their heads above water when swimming.

Mayan artists carved statues of jaguars, including a two-headed throne found at the ancient Mayan city of Uxmal in Mexico.

Status

The International Union for Conservation of Nature (IUCN) has classified the jaguar as a "near threatened" species. However, unless more is done to protect these animals, their conservation status may soon change to "vulnerable." That would mean they are at greater risk of becoming extinct in nature.

Until about 100 years ago, jaguars still commonly lived as far north as California, New Mexico, and Arizona, as well as in Texas. In South America, their range extended to southern Argentina. Today, there are almost no jaguars left in the United States. Most jaguars are now found in the Amazon region. In Mexico, Central America, and other parts of South America, there are fewer jaguars than in the past, and jaguars are found only in parts of their former range. Jaguars now live in only about 40 percent of their former habitats.

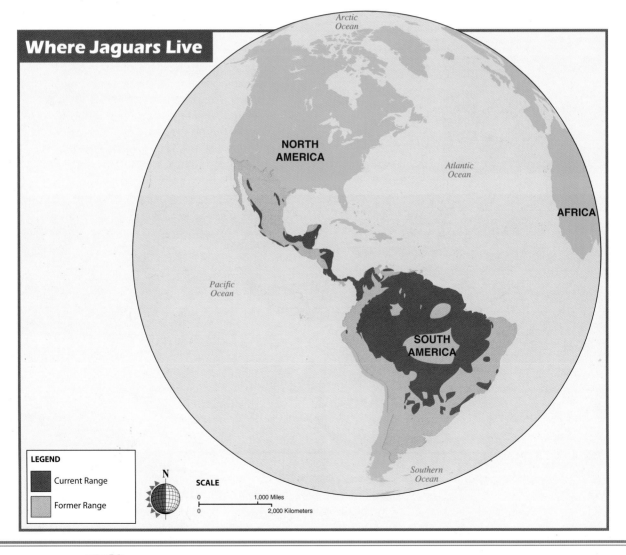

Where Jaguars Live

LEGEND

Current Range

Former Range

Jaguars are sometimes found resting on tree branches.

Clearing forests where jaguars live in order to create farmland is a major problem in Central and South America, where the human population is estimated to doublé every 25 years.

Animals on the Brink

Decline in Population

Hunting and habitat loss have caused a major decline in jaguar populations. Large numbers of jaguars were once taken every year for their fur. Even now that most fur trading is illegal, many jaguars are still hunted for sport and to protect livestock. In some countries where jaguars are protected by law, **poaching** is common. In other countries, jaguars are not even protected by law.

Jaguars are hunted by many different methods. They are often chased by specially trained dogs until they climb a tree to escape. Once in a tree, a jaguar is an easy target for hunters. Another common hunting technique is to wait in ambush near an animal that a jaguar has taken for food. Hunters also use a hollow gourd to make a noise that sounds like a jaguar. This often attracts a jaguar to the area. The hunters can take the cat as it arrives to investigate. Some hunters leave poisoned bait for jaguars to eat.

Today, the biggest threat to jaguars is not hunting but habitat loss. Much of the jaguar's habitat is in tropical forest areas that are being destroyed. Habitat loss is often the result of an increase in the human population in a region. As the population increases, people need to clear more land on which to live.

As land is cleared for villages, crops, and livestock, jaguars are pushed into smaller and smaller areas of land. In each area, a small population of jaguars becomes isolated from other jaguar populations by land that is not suitable for jaguars. Jaguars cannot hunt properly in these isolated areas, and they sometimes cannot find mates. When they are seen near farms, people, or domestic animals, they may be shot.

From an Expert

"If we do not preserve jaguars, they will be converted like our rainforests and finally ourselves, into dust and smoke."
- Rafael Hoogesteijn

Rafael Hoogesteijn is a veterinarian and a zoologist who has long been involved in research on jaguars in Venezuela. He is coauthor of a book titled *The Jaguar.*

Back from the Brink

In 1973, jaguars were put on Appendix 1 of the Convention on International Trade in Endangered Species of Wild Fauna and Flora, known as CITES. This means that the trading of jaguars or jaguar parts, such as skins, can occur only under strict regulations. It also means that commercial trading is banned.

Some countries are not members of CITES and do not follow its rules. In countries such as Brazil, Costa Rica, Guatemala, Mexico, and Peru, hunting is allowed if the jaguar is considered a problem animal. A problem animal is generally one that is often seen near human populations.

International and local conservation groups are working with the governments of countries that have jaguar populations to ensure the survival of the species. One such group, the Wildlife Conservation Society (WCS), also works closely with people in communities that are near jaguar habitats. By educating people about jaguars and helping local ranchers better manage and protect their livestock, the WCS is trying to protect jaguar populations found in Central and South America.

To learn more about jaguars and what can be done to protect them, contact:

Wildlife Conservation Society
2300 Southern Boulevard
Bronx, NY 10460

International Union for Conservation of Nature
28 rue Mauverney
CH-1196 Gland
Switzerland

Organizations, governments, and concerned people around the world are working hard to ensure the survival of jaguars in their natural habitats.

Activity

Debating helps people think about ideas thoughtfully and carefully. When people debate, two sides take a different viewpoint on a subject. Each side takes turns presenting arguments to support its view.

Use the Take a Stand sections found throughout this book as a starting point for debate topics. Organize your friends or classmates into two teams. One team will argue in favor of the topic, and the other will argue against. Each team should research the issue thoroughly using reliable sources of information, including books, scientific journals, and trustworthy websites. Take notes of important facts that support your side of the debate. Prepare your argument using these facts to support your opinion.

During the debate, the members of each team are given a set amount of time to make their arguments. The team arguing the For side goes first. They have five minutes to present their case. All members of the team should participate equally. Then, the team arguing the Against side presents its arguments. Each team should take notes of the main points the other team argues.

After both teams have made their arguments, they get three minutes to prepare their rebuttals. Teams review their notes from the previous round. The teams focus on trying to disprove each of the main points made by the other team using solid facts. Each team gets three minutes to make its rebuttal. The team arguing the Against side goes first. Students and teachers watching the debate serve as judges. They should try to judge the debate fairly using a standard score sheet, such as the example below.

Criteria	Rate: 1-10	Sample Comments
1. Were the arguments well organized?	8	logical arguments, easy to follow
2. Did team members participate equally?	9	divided time evenly between members
3. Did team members speak loudly and clearly?	3	some members were difficult to hear
4. Were rebuttals specific to the other team's arguments?	6	rebuttals were specific, more facts needed
5. Was respect shown for the other team?	10	all members showed respect to the other team

1. Which two other cat species are bigger than jaguars?

2. How long do jaguar cubs stay with their mother?

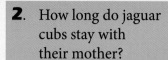

3. What is the name for the black-outlined circles seen on a jaguar's fur?

4. During which part of the day are jaguars most active?

5. How does a jaguar display submission?

6. True or False: The jaguar's ancestors were bigger than the jaguars of today.

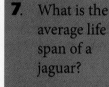

7. What is the average life span of a jaguar?

8. What are three things jaguars do to mark their territory?

9. What are the two main factors that have led to the decline in jaguar populations?

10. What is the jaguar's biggest competitor?

Answers:
1. lions and tigers 2. two years 3. rosettes 4. dusk 5. by lying on its back 6. true. The ancestors of jaguars were about 20 percent bigger than jaguars living today. 7. 10 to 12 years in nature and 20 years in captivity 8. They leave scrape marks, scratch tree bark, and use scent marks. 9. hunting and habitat loss 10. humans

Key Words

adaptations: changes made to fit into a certain environment

canine: a pointed tooth

carnivores: animals that eat mainly the flesh and body parts of other animals

domestic: relates to animals that have been tamed for the benefit of humans

ecosystems: communities of living things and resources

endangered: in danger of becoming extinct, or no longer surviving in the world

extinct: no longer surviving in the world

family: one of eight major ranks used to classify animals, between order and genus

food web: connecting food chains that show how energy moves from one living organism to another through diet

gestation period: the length of time a female is pregnant with young

habitat: a place where animals live, grow, and raise their young

home range: the entire area in which an individual jaguar lives

litter: the number of babies a mother animal gives birth to at one time

mammals: warm-blooded animals that have hair or fur and nurse their young

melanistic: a jaguar with black fur

nurse: when a mammal provides its young with mother's milk

order: one of eight major ranks used to classify animals, between class and family

organisms: forms of life

poaching: a type of hunting that is not legal

prey: animals that are hunted and eaten by other animals

retractable claws: claws that can be pulled back into the paw when not in use

scent marks: areas where an animal leaves a scent to let other animals know it is in the area

scrapes: a possible form of cat communication, where a cat makes scratching marks on the ground with its back feet

species: groups of individuals with common characteristics

threatened: at risk of becoming endangered

vocalizations: sounds made by animals

Index

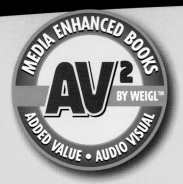

Log on to www.av2books.com

AV² by Weigl brings you media enhanced books that support active learning. Go to www.av2books.com, and enter the special code found on page 2 of this book. You will gain access to enriched and enhanced content that supplements and complements this book. Content includes video, audio, weblinks, quizzes, a slide show, and activities.

AV² Online Navigation

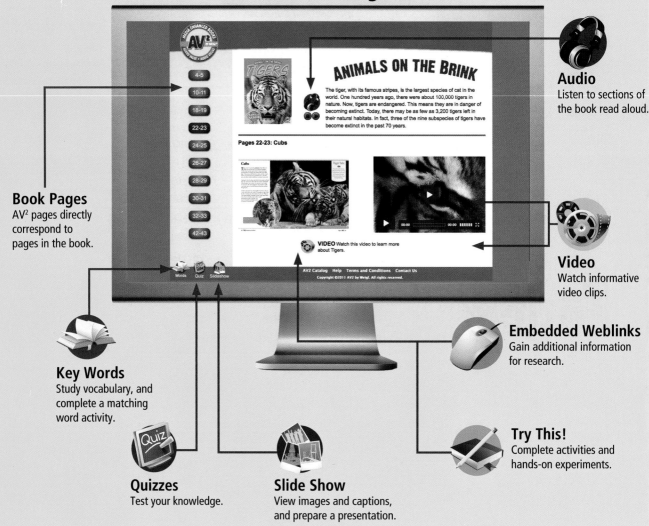

Book Pages
AV² pages directly correspond to pages in the book.

Key Words
Study vocabulary, and complete a matching word activity.

Quizzes
Test your knowledge.

Slide Show
View images and captions, and prepare a presentation.

Audio
Listen to sections of the book read aloud.

Video
Watch informative video clips.

Embedded Weblinks
Gain additional information for research.

Try This!
Complete activities and hands-on experiments.

AV² was built to bridge the gap between print and digital. We encourage you to tell us what you like and what you want to see in the future.

Sign up to be an AV² Ambassador at www.av2books.com/ambassador.

Due to the dynamic nature of the Internet, some of the URLs and activities provided as part of AV² by Weigl may have changed or ceased to exist. AV² by Weigl accepts no responsibility for any such changes. All media enhanced books are regularly monitored to update addresses and sites in a timely manner. Contact AV² by Weigl at 1-866-649-3445 or av2books@weigl.com with any questions, comments, or feedback.